K. CONNORS

C Sharp Programming

The Ultimate Guide to Building Robust, Efficient, and Scalable Applications

Copyright © 2024 by K. Connors

All rights reserved. No part of this publication may be reproduced, stored or transmitted in any form or by any means, electronic, mechanical, photocopying, recording, scanning, or otherwise without written permission from the publisher. It is illegal to copy this book, post it to a website, or distribute it by any other means without permission.

First edition

This book was professionally typeset on Reedsy. Find out more at reedsy.com

Contents

Introduction: The Journey to Mastering C#	1
Chapter 1: Getting Started with C#	6
Chapter 2: Variables, Data Types, and Operators	14
Chapter 3: Control Structures	20
Chapter 4: Methods and Functions	28
Chapter 5: Object-Oriented Programming in C#	35
Chapter 6: Arrays and Collections	45
Chapter 7: Exception Handling	51
Chapter 8: File I/O and Streams	59
Chapter 9: Asynchronous Programming	66
Chapter 10: Advanced Topics and Best Practices	73
Conclusion: Your Next Steps in C# Mastery	83

Introduction: The Journey to Mastering C#

Welcome to the adventure of mastering C#, a language that's both a powerhouse in the programming world and a joy to work with. Whether you're here to jumpstart your career, dive into game development, or simply challenge yourself with a new skill, this book is your guide.

First, let's talk about what C# is. Pronounced "C-sharp," this language was developed by Microsoft as part of the .NET initiative. Over the years, it has grown to be one of the most popular and versatile programming languages available. Its design blends the best elements from other languages like C++ and Java, creating a user-friendly yet powerful tool for developers. C# is used for a myriad of applications: web development, mobile apps, desktop software, games, and more. Essentially, mastering C# opens a multitude of doors in the tech world.

One of the standout features of C# is its simplicity and productivity. This language was designed with developers in mind, making it easier to learn and use. It avoids the pitfalls and complexities of older languages while incorporating modern features that enhance productivity. This makes it an excellent choice for beginners and experienced programmers alike.

Versatility is another hallmark of C#. You can use it to create almost any type of application you can think of. Building dynamic websites? C# is a solid choice. Creating mobile apps? C# has robust support. Developing games?

Thanks to its integration with the Unity game engine, C# is a top pick. This flexibility is not only practical but also incredibly exciting, offering endless possibilities for what you can create.

Now, let's delve into the .NET ecosystem, the environment where C# truly shines. .NET is a free, cross-platform framework that supports multiple programming languages, with C# being its crown jewel. One of the key advantages of .NET is that you can write your code once and run it anywhere—Windows, Linux, macOS, you name it. This cross-platform capability is a game-changer, particularly in today's diverse tech landscape. The .NET framework also includes a vast library of pre-built code, which can significantly speed up development. Whether you're dealing with file I/O, database operations, or web services, .NET has tools that can help you accomplish your tasks more efficiently.

To get started with C#, you'll need to set up your development environment. This might sound daunting, but it's actually quite straightforward. The primary tool for C# development is Visual Studio, an Integrated Development Environment (IDE) that supports code editing, debugging, and version control, all within a user-friendly interface. Visual Studio is packed with features designed to make your life easier, from IntelliSense, which provides intelligent code completions, to powerful debugging tools that help you track down and fix issues quickly. If you prefer a lighter tool, Visual Studio Code is an excellent alternative. It's a versatile, lightweight editor that's perfect for writing C# code and much more.

Now, let's take a closer look at C# itself. One of the first things you'll notice is its readability. The syntax is clean and straightforward, making it easier to learn and understand. This is particularly beneficial if you're new to programming, as it allows you to focus on learning core concepts without getting bogged down by complex syntax. Even though C# is easy to read and write, it doesn't compromise on power. It's a fully-featured, object-oriented language that supports modern programming paradigms and practices.

INTRODUCTION: THE JOURNEY TO MASTERING C#

Throughout this book, we'll cover everything you need to know to become proficient in C#. We'll start with the basics, such as variables, data types, and operators. Understanding these foundational elements is crucial, as they form the building blocks for more complex concepts. Variables are essentially storage containers for data, while data types specify what kind of data a variable can hold. Operators allow you to perform various operations on data, such as arithmetic calculations or comparisons.

Next, we'll move on to control structures, which are constructs that control the flow of your program. These include conditional statements like if, else if, and else, which allow you to execute different blocks of code based on certain conditions. Loops, such as for, while, and do-while loops, enable you to repeat a block of code multiple times. Understanding control structures is essential for writing efficient and effective programs.

Methods and functions are another key area we'll explore. These are blocks of code that perform specific tasks and can be called from other parts of your program. Methods help you organize your code, making it more modular and easier to manage. We'll cover how to define methods, pass parameters, and return values. We'll also discuss method overloading, which allows you to create multiple methods with the same name but different parameters, providing greater flexibility in how you use them.

Object-oriented programming (OOP) is a major focus in C#. OOP is a programming paradigm based on the concept of objects, which are instances of classes. Classes define the properties and behaviors of objects, encapsulating data and functions together. OOP principles like encapsulation, inheritance, and polymorphism help you write code that is more organized, reusable, and maintainable. We'll dive deep into these concepts, explaining how to create classes and objects, how to use inheritance to create hierarchies of classes, and how to achieve polymorphism through method overriding and interfaces.

Arrays and collections are essential for managing groups of related data.

Arrays are fixed-size collections of elements, while collections are more flexible and come in various types, such as lists, dictionaries, queues, and stacks. We'll discuss how to work with both arrays and collections, and we'll introduce LINQ (Language Integrated Query), a powerful tool for querying and manipulating data.

Exception handling is another critical topic. In the real world, things don't always go as planned, and your code needs to be able to handle unexpected situations gracefully. Exception handling allows you to catch and manage errors in a controlled way, preventing your program from crashing and providing useful feedback to the user. We'll cover try-catch-finally blocks, custom exceptions, and best practices for effective error handling.

File I/O and streams are essential for working with external data. Whether you're reading from or writing to files, understanding how to handle file operations is crucial. We'll explore how to work with files and streams, as well as how to serialize and deserialize objects, allowing you to save and retrieve complex data structures.

Asynchronous programming is a must-know for modern developers, particularly when working with I/O-bound or CPU-bound operations that can benefit from concurrency. We'll explain the concepts of async and await, how to use tasks for parallel processing, and best practices for writing efficient and responsive asynchronous code.

Finally, we'll delve into advanced topics and best practices. This includes delegates and events, which are key for implementing event-driven programming. We'll also cover lambda expressions, a shorthand syntax for writing anonymous methods, and generics, which allow you to create flexible and type-safe code. Additionally, we'll introduce some common design patterns that can help you solve recurring problems in software design.

Throughout this journey, we'll provide plenty of real-life scenarios and takeaways to help you understand and apply these concepts. Each chapter is designed to build on the knowledge from the previous one, ensuring a smooth and progressive learning curve. By the end of this book, you'll not only have a solid understanding of C#, but you'll also be equipped with the skills and confidence to tackle a wide range of programming challenges.

Now, let's get started on this exciting journey to mastering C#!

Chapter 1: Getting Started with C#

Welcome to the first chapter of your journey into C# programming! We'll start with the basics, but don't worry – we'll keep it fun and engaging. By the end of this chapter, you'll have a solid foundation and be ready to dive into more complex topics.

First things first: a little background. C# was developed by Microsoft in the early 2000s as part of its .NET initiative. The language was designed to be a modern, simple, and object-oriented programming language. It takes the best features from languages like C++ and Java, making it a powerful and versatile tool for developers. C# is used for a myriad of applications: web development, mobile apps, desktop software, games, and more. Essentially, mastering C# opens a multitude of doors in the tech world.

One of the standout features of C# is its readability. The syntax is straightforward, making it easy to learn and understand. This simplicity is particularly beneficial if you're new to programming, as it allows you to focus on learning core concepts without getting bogged down by complex syntax. Yet, despite its simplicity, C# is a fully-featured language that supports modern programming paradigms and practices.

Let's begin with setting up your development environment. The primary tool for C# development is Visual Studio, an Integrated Development Environment (IDE) that supports code editing, debugging, and version control. Visual Studio is packed with features designed to make your life easier, from intelligent code completions (IntelliSense) to powerful debugging tools. If you prefer something lighter, Visual Studio Code is an excellent alternative. It's a versatile, lightweight editor perfect for writing C# code.

Once you've installed Visual Studio or Visual Studio Code, you're ready to start coding. Open your IDE and create a new project. In Visual Studio, select "Create a new project," choose "Console App (.NET Core)," and click "Next." Name your project, choose a location to save it, and click "Create." Visual Studio will set up your project and generate a basic template for you to start with.

Now, let's write your first C# program – the classic "Hello, World!" program. This simple program will print "Hello, World!" to the console. Here's what the code looks like:

```csharp
using System;

namespace HelloWorld
  {
  class Program
  {
  static void Main(string[] args)
  {
  Console.WriteLine("Hello, World!");
  }
  }
  }
```

Let's break this down:

- The 'using System;' line tells the compiler to include the System namespace, which contains fundamental classes and base classes that define commonly-used data types, events, and events.

- A namespace is a way to organize your code and prevent naming conflicts. Think of it as a container for classes and other types.

- This line defines a class named Program. In C#, a class is a blueprint for creating objects.

- The 'Main' method is the entry point of any C# application. When you run your program, the code inside the Main method is executed.

- The 'Console.WriteLine("Hello, World!");' line prints "Hello, World!" to the console.

Run your program by clicking the "Run" button in Visual Studio, or by pressing Ctrl + F5. You should see "Hello, World!" printed in the console window. Congratulations, you've just written your first C# program!

Now that we've covered the basics, let's dive a bit deeper into C# syntax and structure. Understanding these foundational elements is crucial as they form the building blocks for more complex concepts.

Variables and Constants

In programming, variables are used to store data that can change during the execution of a program. In C#, you declare a variable using the following syntax: 'int age = 25;'

In this example, 'int' is the data type of the variable, and 'age' is the name of the variable. The value '25' is assigned to 'age'.

C# supports various data types, including:

- int: Represents an integer.
    - float: Represents a floating-point number.
    - double: Represents a double-precision floating-point number.
    - char: Represents a single character.

- string: Represents a sequence of characters.
- bool: Represents a Boolean value (true or false).

Constants, on the other hand, are variables whose value cannot change once assigned. You declare a constant using the 'const' keyword: 'const int daysInWeek = 7;'

In this example, 'daysInWeek' is a constant with a value of '7'. Attempting to change the value of a constant will result in a compile-time error.

Data Types

Understanding data types is essential in C# programming. Each data type specifies the kind of data a variable can hold and how much memory it will occupy. Here are some common data types in C#:

- int: Represents an integer (e.g., 42), occupying 4 bytes of memory.
  - float: Represents a single-precision floating-point number (e.g., 3.14f), occupying 4 bytes.
  - double: Represents a double-precision floating-point number (e.g., 3.14), occupying 8 bytes.
  - char: Represents a single character (e.g., 'A'), occupying 2 bytes.
  - string: Represents a sequence of characters (e.g., "Hello"), the size depends on the string length.
  - bool: Represents a Boolean value (true or false), occupying 1 byte.

Understanding these data types and their memory implications is crucial for writing efficient and effective C# code.

Operators

Operators are symbols that perform operations on variables and values. C# supports various operators, including:

- Arithmetic operators: + (addition), - (subtraction), * (multiplication), / (division), % (modulus).
  - Relational operators: == (equal to), != (not equal to), > (greater than), < (less than), >= (greater than or equal to), <= (less than or equal to).
  - Logical operators: && (logical AND), || (logical OR), ! (logical NOT).
  - Assignment operators: = (assignment), += (addition assignment), -= (subtraction assignment), *= (multiplication assignment), /= (division assignment).

Here's an example of how you might use some of these operators in a C# program:

```csharp
int a = 10;
int b = 5;

int sum = a + b; // Addition
int difference = a - b; // Subtraction
int product = a * b; // Multiplication
int quotient = a / b; // Division
int remainder = a % b; // Modulus

bool isEqual = (a == b); // Equal to
bool isGreater = (a > b); // Greater than
```

Type Conversion

Sometimes, you'll need to convert a variable from one data type to another. C# supports both implicit and explicit type conversions.

Implicit conversions occur when the conversion is safe and no data will be lost. For example, converting an int to a float:

```csharp
int num = 10;
```

```
float numFloat = num; // Implicit conversion
```

Explicit conversions require a cast, as there's a potential for data loss. For example, converting a float to an int:

```
float numFloat = 10.5f;
    int num = (int)numFloat; // Explicit conversion
```

In this case, num will have a value of 10, as the fractional part is truncated.

Control Structures

Control structures control the flow of your program. The most common control structures are conditional statements and loops.

Conditional statements allow you to execute different blocks of code based on certain conditions. The most common conditional statement is the 'if' statement:

```
int age = 20;

if (age >= 18)
   {
   Console.WriteLine("You are an adult.");
   }
   else
   {
   Console.WriteLine("You are a minor.");
   }
```

Loops allow you to repeat a block of code multiple times. The most common types of loops are for, while, and do-while loops.

A for loop repeats a block of code a specified number of times:

```csharp
for (int i = 0; i < 5; i++)
{
    Console.WriteLine("Iteration: " + i);
}
```

A while loop repeats a block of code as long as a specified condition is true:

```csharp
int i = 0;

while (i < 5)
{
    Console.WriteLine("Iteration: " + i);
    i++;
}
```

A do-while loop is similar to a while loop, but it guarantees that the block of code will be executed at least once:

```csharp
int i = 0;

do
{
    Console.WriteLine("Iteration: " + i);
    i++;
} while (i < 5);
```

Understanding and mastering these control structures will enable you to write efficient and effective C# programs.

By now, you should have a solid understanding of the basics of C# programming. We've covered setting up your development environment, writing and running your first program, and the foundational elements of C# syntax and structure. These concepts are the building blocks for more complex topics that we'll explore in the coming chapters.

Now, with this foundational knowledge in place, you're ready to dive deeper into the world of C# programming.

Chapter 2: Variables, Data Types, and Operators

Alright, now that we've got our feet wet with the basics, it's time to dive a bit deeper into the core elements that make up C# programming. This chapter is all about variables, data types, and operators. These are the building blocks of any program, so understanding them thoroughly is essential.

First up, variables. In programming, variables are used to store data that can change during the execution of a program. Think of variables as containers for data. You give these containers a name, and you can use that name to access the data stored within them. Declaring a variable in C# involves specifying the type of data it will hold and giving it a name.

For instance, if you want to store an integer (a whole number), you would declare it like this: int age = 25;

In this example, int is the data type, age is the variable name, and 25 is the value assigned to the variable. You can change the value of the variable later in the program. For example: age = 30;

C# supports various data types, each designed to hold a specific kind of data. Here are some common data types:

CHAPTER 2: VARIABLES, DATA TYPES, AND OPERATORS

- int: Represents an integer. For example, 42 or -10.
  - float: Represents a floating-point number, which is a number with a decimal point. For example, 3.14f.
  - double: Similar to float but with double the precision. For example, 3.14159265359.
    - char: Represents a single character. For example, 'A' or 'z'.
    - string: Represents a sequence of characters. For example, "Hello, World!".
    - bool: Represents a Boolean value, which can be either true or false.

Each data type serves a specific purpose and has its own set of rules. For example, you can't store a string in an int variable because they're designed to hold different types of data.

Constants are a special type of variable whose value cannot be changed once it's assigned. You declare a constant using the const keyword. For example: const int daysInWeek = 7;

Constants are useful when you have values that should remain the same throughout the execution of your program, like the number of days in a week or the value of pi.

Next, let's talk about operators. Operators are symbols that tell the compiler to perform specific mathematical or logical manipulations. C# supports a variety of operators, and understanding them is key to performing calculations and making decisions in your code.

Arithmetic operators are used to perform basic mathematical operations:

- + (addition): Adds two operands. For example, 5 + 3 equals 8.
  - - (subtraction): Subtracts the second operand from the first. For example, 5 - 3 equals 2.
    - * (multiplication): Multiplies two operands. For example, 5 * 3 equals 15.
    - / (division): Divides the first operand by the second. For example, 6 / 3

equals 2.

- % (modulus): Returns the remainder of a division operation. For example, 5 % 2 equals 1.

These operators are pretty straightforward, but they form the basis of most calculations in your programs.

Relational operators are used to compare two values and return a Boolean value (true or false):

- == (equal to): Checks if two values are equal. For example, 5 == 5 is true.
- != (not equal to): Checks if two values are not equal. For example, 5 != 3 is true.
- > (greater than): Checks if the first value is greater than the second. For example, 5 > 3 is true.
- < (less than): Checks if the first value is less than the second. For example, 3 < 5 is true.
- >= (greater than or equal to): Checks if the first value is greater than or equal to the second. For example, 5 >= 5 is true.
- <= (less than or equal to): Checks if the first value is less than or equal to the second. For example, 3 <= 5 is true.

Logical operators are used to combine multiple Boolean expressions:

- && (logical AND): Returns true if both operands are true. For example, (5 > 3) && (3 > 1) is true.
- || (logical OR): Returns true if at least one operand is true. For example, (5 > 3) || (3 > 5) is true.
- ! (logical NOT): Reverses the Boolean value. For example, !(5 > 3) is false.

These operators are crucial for making decisions in your programs. You'll often use them in conditional statements, which we'll cover in a later chapter.

CHAPTER 2: VARIABLES, DATA TYPES, AND OPERATORS

Assignment operators are used to assign values to variables. The most basic assignment operator is the equals sign (=), which we've already seen. However, there are also compound assignment operators that perform an operation and assign the result in one step:

- += (addition assignment): Adds the right operand to the left operand and assigns the result to the left operand. For example, a += 3 is equivalent to a = a + 3.
  - -= (subtraction assignment): Subtracts the right operand from the left operand and assigns the result to the left operand. For example, a -= 3 is equivalent to a = a - 3.
  - *= (multiplication assignment): Multiplies the left operand by the right operand and assigns the result to the left operand. For example, a *= 3 is equivalent to a = a * 3.
  - /= (division assignment): Divides the left operand by the right operand and assigns the result to the left operand. For example, a /= 3 is equivalent to a = a / 3.
  - %= (modulus assignment): Performs the modulus operation on the left operand and assigns the result to the left operand. For example, a %= 3 is equivalent to a = a % 3.

Understanding and using these operators effectively can make your code more concise and readable.

Type conversion is another important concept. Sometimes, you'll need to convert a variable from one data type to another. C# supports both implicit and explicit type conversions.

Implicit conversions occur when the conversion is safe and no data will be lost. For example, converting an int to a float:

```
int num = 10;
    float numFloat = num;
```

In this case, the int value is safely converted to a float.

Explicit conversions, also known as casting, are necessary when there is a potential for data loss. For example, converting a float to an int requires an explicit cast:

float numFloat = 10.5f;
    int num = (int)numFloat;

In this case, the float value is converted to an int, and the fractional part is truncated, resulting in a value of 10.

C# also provides methods for converting between different data types. For example, the 'Convert' class offers a range of methods for converting data types, such as 'Convert.ToInt32()' for converting to an int or 'Convert.ToDouble()' for converting to a double.

Understanding these concepts—variables, data types, operators, and type conversion—is crucial for writing effective and efficient C# programs. These elements form the foundation of your code, allowing you to perform calculations, make decisions, and manipulate data.

Let's wrap up this chapter with a real-life scenario to put these concepts into context. Suppose you're working on a simple banking application that tracks a user's balance and allows deposits and withdrawals. Here's how you might use variables, data types, and operators in this scenario:

int balance = 1000; // Starting balance

int deposit = 200;
    balance += deposit; // Add deposit to balance

int withdrawal = 150;

CHAPTER 2: VARIABLES, DATA TYPES, AND OPERATORS

balance -= withdrawal; // Subtract withdrawal from balance

bool isBalancePositive = balance > 0; // Check if balance is positive

Console.WriteLine("Balance: " + balance);
   Console.WriteLine("Is balance positive? " + isBalancePositive);

In this example, we declare variables to store the balance, deposit amount, and withdrawal amount. We use arithmetic operators to update the balance and a relational operator to check if the balance is positive. Finally, we print the balance and the result of the check.

By understanding and effectively using variables, data types, operators, and type conversions, you can build the foundation for more complex and powerful programs. As we continue our journey through C# programming, these core concepts will become second nature, enabling you to tackle a wide range of programming challenges with confidence.

Chapter 3: Control Structures

Welcome to the world of control structures in C#. Control structures are essential components that dictate the flow of your program. They allow you to make decisions, execute code repeatedly, and manage how different parts of your code interact with each other. Understanding control structures is crucial for writing dynamic and responsive programs.

Let's start with conditional statements. These are used to perform different actions based on different conditions. The most common conditional statement in C# is the 'if' statement. An 'if' statement evaluates a condition and executes a block of code if the condition is true.

Here's a basic example of an 'if' statement in action:

```
int number = 10;

if (number > 5)
   {
   Console.WriteLine("The number is greater than 5.");
   }
```

In this example, the condition 'number > 5' is evaluated. Since the condition is true, the code inside the curly braces is executed, and "The number is greater than 5." is printed to the console.

CHAPTER 3: CONTROL STRUCTURES

You can extend the functionality of the 'if' statement by using 'else' and 'else if'. The 'else' statement allows you to specify a block of code to execute if the condition in the 'if' statement is false. The 'else if' statement lets you check multiple conditions.

Here's an example that demonstrates the use of 'else' and 'else if':

```
int number = 10;

if (number > 10)
    {
    Console.WriteLine("The number is greater than 10.");
    }
    else if (number == 10)
    {
    Console.WriteLine("The number is equal to 10.");
    }
    else
    {
    Console.WriteLine("The number is less than 10.");
    }
```

In this example, the program checks if 'number' is greater than 10. If not, it checks if 'number' is equal to 10. If neither condition is true, the code inside the 'else' block is executed. This structure allows you to handle multiple conditions and execute different code blocks based on the result of those conditions.

Next, let's explore the 'switch' statement. The 'switch' statement is used to select one of many code blocks to execute. It evaluates an expression and executes the code block associated with the matching 'case' label. If no 'case' matches, the code in the 'default' block is executed.

Here's an example of a 'switch' statement:

```csharp
int dayOfWeek = 3;

switch (dayOfWeek)
    {
    case 1:
    Console.WriteLine("Monday");
    break;
    case 2:
    Console.WriteLine("Tuesday");
    break;
    case 3:
    Console.WriteLine("Wednesday");
    break;
    case 4:
    Console.WriteLine("Thursday");
    break;
    case 5:
    Console.WriteLine("Friday");
    break;
    case 6:
    Console.WriteLine("Saturday");
    break;
    case 7:
    Console.WriteLine("Sunday");
    break;
    default:
    Console.WriteLine("Invalid day");
    break;
    }
```

In this example, the value of 'dayOfWeek' is compared against each 'case' label. Since 'dayOfWeek' is 3, the code block for 'case 3' is executed, and "Wednesday" is printed to the console. The 'break' statement is used to exit the 'switch' statement once a matching case is found.

Control structures also include loops, which allow you to execute a block of code repeatedly. The most common types of loops in C# are 'for', 'while', and 'do-while'.

The 'for' loop is used to execute a block of code a specific number of times. It consists of three parts: initialization, condition, and iteration. The initialization sets up the loop variable, the condition is checked before each iteration, and the iteration updates the loop variable.

Here's an example of a 'for' loop:

```
for (int i = 0; i < 5; i++)
  {
  Console.WriteLine("Iteration: " + i);
  }
```

In this example, the loop variable 'i' is initialized to 0. The condition 'i < 5' is checked before each iteration, and 'i' is incremented by 1 after each iteration. The loop executes 5 times, printing the value of 'i' each time.

The 'while' loop executes a block of code as long as a specified condition is true. The condition is checked before each iteration, and if it evaluates to false, the loop is exited.

Here's an example of a 'while' loop:

```
int i = 0;

while (i < 5)
  {
  Console.WriteLine("Iteration: " + i);
```

```
i++;
}
```

In this example, the loop variable 'i' is initialized to 0. The condition 'i < 5' is checked before each iteration, and 'i' is incremented by 1 after each iteration. The loop executes 5 times, printing the value of 'i' each time.

The 'do-while' loop is similar to the 'while' loop, but the condition is checked after each iteration. This guarantees that the code block is executed at least once.

Here's an example of a 'do-while' loop:

```
int i = 0;

do
  {
  Console.WriteLine("Iteration: " + i);
  i++;
  } while (i < 5);
```

In this example, the loop variable 'i' is initialized to 0. The code block is executed, and 'i' is incremented by 1. The condition 'i < 5' is then checked, and if true, the loop continues. This process repeats until the condition evaluates to false.

Understanding these loops is crucial for tasks that require repetitive operations, such as iterating through collections or processing items in a list.

C# also supports 'foreach' loops, which are specifically designed for iterating through collections. The 'foreach' loop simplifies the process of traversing elements in an array or collection.

Here's an example of a 'foreach' loop:

```
int[] numbers = { 1, 2, 3, 4, 5 };

foreach (int number in numbers)
    {
    Console.WriteLine("Number: " + number);
    }
```

In this example, the 'foreach' loop iterates through each element in the 'numbers' array and prints it to the console. The loop variable 'number' takes on the value of each element in the array, one at a time.

Control structures in C# also include jump statements, which allow you to change the flow of execution. The most common jump statements are 'break', 'continue', and 'goto'.

The 'break' statement is used to exit a loop or switch statement prematurely. It immediately terminates the enclosing loop or switch statement and transfers control to the next statement following the loop or switch.

Here's an example of the 'break' statement in a loop:

```
for (int i = 0; i < 10; i++)
    {
    if (i == 5)
    {
    break;
    }
    Console.WriteLine("Iteration: " + i);
    }
```

In this example, the loop iterates from 0 to 9. However, when 'i' reaches 5, the 'break' statement is executed, and the loop is terminated.

The 'continue' statement is used to skip the current iteration of a loop and proceed with the next iteration. It transfers control to the next iteration of the enclosing loop.

Here's an example of the 'continue' statement:

```
for (int i = 0; i < 10; i++)
    {
    if (i % 2 == 0)
    {
    continue;
    }
    Console.WriteLine("Odd number: " + i);
    }
```

In this example, the loop iterates from 0 to 9. When 'i' is an even number, the 'continue' statement is executed, and the current iteration is skipped. The loop then proceeds with the next iteration.

The 'goto' statement transfers control to a labeled statement within the same function. It can be used to jump to a specific point in the code, but it should be used sparingly as it can make the code difficult to read and maintain.

Here's an example of the 'goto' statement:

```
int number = 10;

if (number > 5)
    {
    goto Label;
    }
```

Console.WriteLine("This will be skipped.");

Label:
  Console.WriteLine("This will be executed.");

In this example, the 'goto' statement transfers control to the labeled statement 'Label', skipping the intermediate code. While the 'goto' statement can be useful in certain situations, it's generally recommended to use other control structures for better code readability.

Control structures are essential for writing dynamic and responsive programs. They allow you to make decisions, execute code repeatedly, and manage the flow of your program. By mastering conditional statements, loops, and jump statements, you can create programs that are both flexible and powerful. These concepts form the backbone of most programming tasks, enabling you to tackle a wide range of challenges with confidence and precision.

Chapter 4: Methods and Functions

Welcome to the world of methods and functions in C#. If control structures are the skeleton of your program, methods and functions are its muscles. They give your code structure, organization, and reusability. By the end of this chapter, you'll understand how to create and use methods effectively, making your programs more modular and easier to manage.

Let's start with the basics. In C#, a method is a block of code that performs a specific task. You can think of a method as a small program within a program. Methods help you organize your code into manageable chunks, making it easier to read, understand, and maintain.

To define a method, you need to specify its access level, return type, name, and parameters. Here's a basic example:

```
public void Greet()
  {
  Console.WriteLine("Hello, world!");
  }
```

In this example, we define a method named 'Greet' with a 'public' access level, a 'void' return type, and no parameters. The 'public' access level means that the method can be called from outside the class it belongs to. The 'void' return type means that the method does not return any value. Inside the method, we use 'Console.WriteLine' to print a message to the console.

To call a method, you simply use its name followed by parentheses. For example:

Greet();

When this line of code is executed, the 'Greet' method is called, and the message "Hello, world!" is printed to the console.

Methods can also take parameters, which are values you pass to the method to influence its behavior. Parameters are defined inside the parentheses in the method definition. Here's an example:

```
public void Greet(string name)
   {
   Console.WriteLine("Hello, " + name + "!");
   }
```

In this example, the 'Greet' method takes a single parameter of type 'string' named 'name'. Inside the method, we use 'Console.WriteLine' to print a personalized greeting message to the console. To call this method, you need to provide an argument for the 'name' parameter:

Greet("Alice");

When this line of code is executed, the 'Greet' method is called with the argument "Alice", and the message "Hello, Alice!" is printed to the console.

Methods can also return values. To specify the return type of a method, you replace 'void' with the appropriate data type. The method must then use the 'return' statement to return a value of that type. Here's an example:

```csharp
public int Add(int a, int b)
{
    return a + b;
}
```

In this example, the 'Add' method takes two parameters of type 'int' named 'a' and 'b'. It returns an 'int' value, which is the sum of 'a' and 'b'. To call this method and store the result in a variable, you can use the following code:

```csharp
int result = Add(3, 5);
```

When this line of code is executed, the 'Add' method is called with the arguments 3 and 5, and the result (8) is stored in the 'result' variable.

Methods can also be overloaded, which means you can define multiple methods with the same name but different parameters. This allows you to create methods that perform similar tasks but with different inputs. Here's an example:

```csharp
public int Add(int a, int b)
{
    return a + b;
}

public double Add(double a, double b)
{
    return a + b;
}
```

In this example, we define two 'Add' methods: one that takes 'int' parameters and another that takes 'double' parameters. When you call the 'Add' method, the compiler determines which method to use based on the types of the arguments you provide:

CHAPTER 4: METHODS AND FUNCTIONS

```
int intResult = Add(3, 5); // Calls the first Add method
    double doubleResult = Add(3.5, 5.5); // Calls the second Add method
```

This feature, known as method overloading, enhances the flexibility and reusability of your methods.

Now, let's discuss the concept of recursion. Recursion occurs when a method calls itself. This technique can be very powerful for solving certain types of problems, particularly those that can be broken down into smaller, similar problems. However, recursion must be used carefully to avoid infinite loops and stack overflow errors.

Here's a classic example of a recursive method: calculating the factorial of a number. The factorial of a number 'n' is the product of all positive integers less than or equal to 'n' and is denoted by 'n¡. For example, '5¡ is '5 * 4 * 3 * 2 * 1', which equals '120'.

```
public int Factorial(int n)
  {
  if (n == 0)
  {
  return 1;
  }
  else
  {
  return n * Factorial(n - 1);
  }
  }
```

In this example, the 'Factorial' method calculates the factorial of a given number 'n'. If 'n' is '0', the method returns '1' (since '0¡ is '1'). Otherwise, the method calls itself with 'n - 1' and multiplies the result by 'n'. This process continues until 'n' reaches '0', at which point the recursion stops, and the final result is returned.

Understanding how and when to use recursion is an important skill, but it's not always the best solution. Iterative solutions (using loops) can sometimes be more efficient and easier to understand. Use recursion judiciously and ensure that each recursive call brings you closer to a base case, which terminates the recursion.

Let's now talk about access modifiers, which control the visibility of your methods. The most common access modifiers are 'public', 'private', and 'protected'.

- 'public': The method is accessible from any other class.
    - 'private': The method is accessible only within the class it is defined.
    - 'protected': The method is accessible within its class and by derived class instances.

Using access modifiers properly is crucial for encapsulation, which is one of the fundamental principles of object-oriented programming. Encapsulation ensures that the internal state of an object is hidden from the outside world and can only be accessed or modified through methods. This prevents unauthorized access and modification, making your code more robust and maintainable.

Here's an example of using access modifiers:

```
public class Calculator
    {
    public int Add(int a, int b)
    {
    return a + b;
    }
```

```
private int Subtract(int a, int b)
  {
  return a - b;
  }
}
```

In this example, the 'Add' method is 'public', so it can be called from outside the 'Calculator' class. The 'Subtract' method is 'private', so it can only be called within the 'Calculator' class.

Finally, let's discuss the concept of static methods. A static method belongs to the class itself rather than to instances of the class. This means you can call a static method without creating an object of the class. Static methods are often used for utility functions that do not depend on instance data.

Here's an example of a static method:

```
public class MathUtilities
  {
  public static int Square(int number)
  {
  return number * number;
  }
}
```

In this example, the 'Square' method is static, so it can be called directly on the 'MathUtilities' class:

```
int result = MathUtilities.Square(4);
```

When this line of code is executed, the 'Square' method is called with the argument '4', and the result ('16') is stored in the 'result' variable.

Static methods can be very useful, but they should be used judiciously. Overuse of static methods can lead to code that is difficult to test and maintain. As a general rule, use static methods for operations that do not depend on instance data and do not require overriding in derived classes.

In conclusion, methods and functions are essential tools for organizing and structuring your code. By understanding how to define, call, and overload methods, you can create programs that are modular, reusable, and easy to maintain. Whether you're using simple methods to perform basic tasks or complex recursive methods to solve intricate problems, mastering methods and functions will significantly enhance your programming skills.

Chapter 5: Object-Oriented Programming in C#

Welcome to the world of object-oriented programming (OOP) in C#. OOP is a programming paradigm that uses objects and classes to create models based on the real world. This approach allows you to organize code in a way that is modular, reusable, and easy to maintain. In this chapter, we'll explore the core concepts of OOP and see how they can be applied in C#.

First, let's define some key terms. An **object** is an instance of a class, and a **class** is a blueprint for creating objects. Think of a class as a template that defines the properties and behaviors of objects. Each object created from a class can have its own unique values for the properties defined by the class.

Classes and Objects

To define a class in C#, you use the 'class' keyword followed by the class name. Inside the class, you can define fields (variables), properties, methods, and events. Here is a simple example of a class definition:

```
class Car
   {
   public string Make { get; set; }
   public string Model { get; set; }
```

```
public int Year { get; set; }

public void Drive()
   {
   Console.WriteLine("The car is driving.");
   }
}
```

In this example, we define a 'Car' class with three properties: 'Make', 'Model', and 'Year'. We also define a method 'Drive', which prints a message to the console. The properties are defined using the '{ get; set; }' syntax, which creates auto-implemented properties. This syntax is a shorthand way of defining properties without explicitly declaring the backing fields.

To create an object from a class, you use the 'new' keyword followed by the class name. Here is an example:

```
Car myCar = new Car();
   myCar.Make = "Toyota";
   myCar.Model = "Camry";
   myCar.Year = 2020;

myCar.Drive();
```

In this example, we create an object 'myCar' from the 'Car' class. We then set the values for the 'Make', 'Model', and 'Year' properties and call the 'Drive' method.

Encapsulation

Encapsulation is one of the fundamental principles of OOP. It refers to the bundling of data (fields) and methods (functions) that operate on the data into a single unit, or class. Encapsulation helps to protect the internal state of an object from unintended or harmful changes. It is achieved by making fields private and providing public properties or methods to access and modify the fields.

Here is an example of encapsulation:

```
class BankAccount
  {
  private decimal balance;

public decimal Balance
  {
  get { return balance; }
  private set { balance = value; }
  }

public void Deposit(decimal amount)
  {
  if (amount > 0)
  {
  Balance += amount;
  }
  }

public void Withdraw(decimal amount)
  {
  if (amount > 0 && amount <= Balance)
  {
  Balance -= amount;
  }
  }
  }
```

In this example, the 'balance' field is private, meaning it cannot be accessed directly from outside the 'BankAccount' class. Instead, we provide a public property 'Balance' with a private setter and two public methods 'Deposit' and 'Withdraw' to modify the balance. This ensures that the balance cannot be set to an invalid value.

Inheritance

Inheritance is another core principle of OOP. It allows you to create a new class that is based on an existing class. The new class, called a derived class, inherits the properties and methods of the existing class, called the base class. Inheritance promotes code reuse and establishes a natural hierarchical relationship between classes.

Here is an example of inheritance:

```
class Vehicle
{
public string Color { get; set; }

public void Start()
{
Console.WriteLine("The vehicle is starting.");
}
}

class Motorcycle : Vehicle
{
public int EngineSize { get; set; }

public void RevEngine()
{
Console.WriteLine("The motorcycle engine is revving.");
```

```
}
}
```

In this example, the 'Vehicle' class is the base class, and the 'Motorcycle' class is the derived class. The 'Motorcycle' class inherits the 'Color' property and the 'Start' method from the 'Vehicle' class. It also defines its own property 'EngineSize' and method 'RevEngine'.

To create an object of the derived class and access both the inherited and new members, you can do the following:

```
Motorcycle myMotorcycle = new Motorcycle();
   myMotorcycle.Color = "Red";
   myMotorcycle.EngineSize = 600;

myMotorcycle.Start();
   myMotorcycle.RevEngine();
```

In this example, we create an object 'myMotorcycle' from the 'Motorcycle' class. We set the values for the 'Color' and 'EngineSize' properties, call the inherited 'Start' method, and call the 'RevEngine' method.

Polymorphism

Polymorphism is the ability of different classes to be treated as instances of the same class through inheritance. It allows you to define methods in the base class and override them in the derived class to provide specific implementations. Polymorphism enables you to write code that can work with objects of different types in a uniform way.

Here is an example of polymorphism:

```
class Animal
```

```csharp
    {
        public virtual void Speak()
        {
            Console.WriteLine("The animal makes a sound.");
        }
    }

class Dog : Animal
    {
        public override void Speak()
        {
            Console.WriteLine("The dog barks.");
        }
    }

class Cat : Animal
    {
        public override void Speak()
        {
            Console.WriteLine("The cat meows.");
        }
    }
```

In this example, the 'Animal' class defines a virtual method 'Speak', which can be overridden in derived classes. The 'Dog' and 'Cat' classes override the 'Speak' method to provide their specific implementations.

To demonstrate polymorphism, you can create a list of 'Animal' objects and call the 'Speak' method on each object:

```csharp
List<Animal> animals = new List<Animal>
    {
        new Dog(),
```

```
  new Cat()
};

foreach (Animal animal in animals)
{
  animal.Speak();
}
```

In this example, we create a list of 'Animal' objects containing a 'Dog' and a 'Cat'. We then iterate through the list and call the 'Speak' method on each object. The correct method for each object is called based on its actual type, demonstrating polymorphism.

Abstraction

Abstraction is the process of hiding the implementation details and showing only the essential features of an object. It allows you to focus on what an object does rather than how it does it. Abstraction is achieved in C# through abstract classes and interfaces.

An abstract class is a class that cannot be instantiated and may contain abstract methods, which are methods without implementation. Derived classes must provide implementations for the abstract methods.

Here is an example of an abstract class:

```
abstract class Shape
  {
  public abstract double GetArea();
  }

class Circle : Shape
  {
```

```csharp
public double Radius { get; set; }

public override double GetArea()
    {
    return Math.PI * Radius * Radius;
    }
}

class Rectangle : Shape
    {
    public double Width { get; set; }
    public double Height { get; set; }

public override double GetArea()
    {
    return Width * Height;
    }
}
```

In this example, the 'Shape' class is an abstract class with an abstract method 'GetArea'. The 'Circle' and 'Rectangle' classes derive from 'Shape' and provide their specific implementations of the 'GetArea' method.

An interface is a contract that defines a set of methods and properties that a class must implement. Interfaces provide a way to achieve multiple inheritance, as a class can implement multiple interfaces.

Here is an example of an interface:

```csharp
interface IMovable
    {
    void Move();
    }
```

```csharp
class Car : IMovable
  {
  public void Move()
  {
  Console.WriteLine("The car is moving.");
  }
  }

class Person : IMovable
  {
  public void Move()
  {
  Console.WriteLine("The person is walking.");
  }
  }
```

In this example, the 'IMovable' interface defines a 'Move' method. The 'Car' and 'Person' classes implement the 'IMovable' interface and provide their specific implementations of the 'Move' method.

To demonstrate the use of interfaces, you can create a list of 'IMovable' objects and call the 'Move' method on each object:

```csharp
List<IMovable> movables = new List<IMovable>
  {
  new Car(),
  new Person()
  };

foreach (IMovable movable in movables)
  {
  movable.Move();
  }
```

In this example, we create a list of 'IMovable' objects containing a 'Car' and a 'Person'. We then iterate through the list and call the 'Move' method on each object. The correct method for each object is called based on its actual type, demonstrating the power of interfaces and abstraction.

Object-oriented programming in C# provides a robust framework for building modular, reusable, and maintainable code. By mastering the concepts of classes, objects, encapsulation, inheritance, polymorphism, and abstraction, you can create complex and dynamic applications that are easy to understand and extend. These principles are the foundation of modern software development and will serve you well as you continue to grow as a programmer.

Chapter 6: Arrays and Collections

Welcome to the realm of arrays and collections in C#. These data structures are the unsung heroes of programming, quietly working behind the scenes to organize and manage data efficiently. Whether you're dealing with a list of numbers, a collection of objects, or a sequence of characters, arrays and collections are your go-to tools. In this chapter, we'll explore the various types of arrays and collections available in C#, how to use them, and their specific advantages.

Let's kick things off with arrays. An array is a fixed-size, ordered collection of elements of the same type. Arrays are handy when you know the number of elements in advance and need to access them using an index. To declare an array in C#, you specify the type of elements it will hold, followed by square brackets. Here's an example:

int[] numbers = new int[5];

In this example, we declare an array named 'numbers' that can hold five integers. Initially, all elements in the array are set to the default value for the specified type (in this case, 0 for integers). You can also initialize an array with specific values:

int[] numbers = { 1, 2, 3, 4, 5 };

Arrays are zero-indexed, meaning the first element has an index of 0, the second element has an index of 1, and so on. To access an element in an array, you use its index:

int firstNumber = numbers[0]; // Accesses the first element
  numbers[2] = 10; // Modifies the third element

While arrays are efficient for fixed-size collections, they have limitations. For instance, you cannot change the size of an array once it's created. This is where collections come into play.

Collections in C# are dynamic data structures that can grow and shrink as needed. The System.Collections and System.Collections.Generic namespaces provide a variety of collection types, each with its own characteristics and use cases. Let's delve into some of the most commonly used collections.

First, we have the List<T> collection. The List<T> class represents a list of objects that can be accessed by index. It provides methods for adding, removing, and searching for elements. The T in List<T> is a placeholder for the type of elements the list will hold. Here's an example:

List<int> numbers = new List<int>();
  numbers.Add(1);
  numbers.Add(2);
  numbers.Add(3);

In this example, we create a List of integers and add three elements to it. Unlike arrays, lists can dynamically grow as you add more elements. You can also remove elements from a list, making it a flexible and versatile data structure. Here's how you might remove an element:

numbers.Remove(2); // Removes the element with value 2

Another useful collection is the Dictionary<TKey, TValue>. A Dictionary is a collection of key-value pairs, where each key is unique. This makes dictionaries perfect for scenarios where you need to associate values with keys and quickly retrieve them. Here's an example:

```
Dictionary<string, int> ages = new Dictionary<string, int>();
    ages.Add("Alice", 30);
    ages.Add("Bob", 25);
```

In this example, we create a Dictionary where the keys are strings (names) and the values are integers (ages). You can access the value associated with a key like this:

```
int aliceAge = ages["Alice"];
```

Dictionaries are highly efficient for lookups, insertions, and deletions, provided you use the keys correctly. You can also check if a key exists before accessing its value:

```
if (ages.ContainsKey("Charlie"))
    {
    int charlieAge = ages["Charlie"];
    }
    else
    {
    Console.WriteLine("Key not found.");
    }
```

Next up is the Queue<T> collection. A Queue is a first-in, first-out (FIFO) collection. Elements are added to the end of the queue and removed from the front. This makes queues ideal for scenarios where you need to process elements in the order they were added. Here's an example:

```csharp
Queue<string> queue = new Queue<string>();
    queue.Enqueue("First");
    queue.Enqueue("Second");
    queue.Enqueue("Third");
```

In this example, we create a Queue of strings and add three elements to it. To remove and return the element at the front of the queue, you use the Dequeue method:

```csharp
string firstElement = queue.Dequeue(); // "First"
```

Queues are great for task scheduling, buffering, and managing sequences of events where order matters.

On the flip side, we have the Stack<T> collection. A Stack is a last-in, first-out (LIFO) collection. Elements are added to the top of the stack and removed from the top. This makes stacks suitable for scenarios where you need to reverse the order of elements or process the most recent element first. Here's an example:

```csharp
Stack<string> stack = new Stack<string>();
    stack.Push("First");
    stack.Push("Second");
    stack.Push("Third");
```

In this example, we create a Stack of strings and add three elements to it. To remove and return the element at the top of the stack, you use the Pop method:

```csharp
string topElement = stack.Pop(); // "Third"
```

Stacks are commonly used for undo mechanisms, parsing expressions, and managing nested structures like method calls.

Another useful collection is the HashSet<T>. A HashSet is an unordered collection of unique elements. It is highly efficient for set operations like union, intersection, and difference. Here's an example:

```
HashSet<int> set = new HashSet<int>();
    set.Add(1);
    set.Add(2);
    set.Add(3);
    set.Add(1); // Duplicate elements are not added
```

In this example, we create a HashSet of integers and add three elements to it. The HashSet automatically handles duplicates, ensuring that each element is unique. You can check for membership, perform set operations, and iterate over the elements:

```
bool containsTwo = set.Contains(2); // True
    set.Remove(3); // Removes the element 3
```

HashSets are perfect for scenarios where uniqueness matters, such as managing user IDs, ensuring no duplicates in a collection, and performing set-based calculations.

Finally, let's talk about LinkedList<T>. A LinkedList is a collection of nodes, where each node contains a value and a reference to the next node. Linked lists allow for efficient insertion and deletion of elements at any position. Here's an example:

```
LinkedList<string> linkedList = new LinkedList<string>();
    linkedList.AddLast("First");
    linkedList.AddLast("Second");
    linkedList.AddLast("Third");
```

In this example, we create a LinkedList of strings and add three elements to it. Linked lists are particularly useful when you need to frequently insert or delete elements at arbitrary positions. You can add elements to the beginning or end, and remove elements from any position:

linkedList.AddFirst("New First"); // Adds to the beginning
linkedList.Remove("Second"); // Removes the element with value "Second"

LinkedLists are ideal for scenarios that require dynamic data structures with frequent insertions and deletions, such as implementing queues, stacks, and other complex data structures.

Understanding the various types of arrays and collections available in C# is crucial for choosing the right data structure for your needs. Arrays provide efficient access and manipulation for fixed-size collections, while collections offer flexibility and dynamic sizing for more complex scenarios. By mastering these data structures, you can write efficient, maintainable, and scalable code that handles a wide range of data management tasks.

Arrays and collections are foundational to effective programming, enabling you to organize, manipulate, and access data efficiently. Whether you're dealing with a simple list of numbers or a complex set of relationships, C# provides the tools you need to manage your data with ease. As you continue to explore and use these data structures, you'll find that they are indispensable in building robust and efficient applications.

Chapter 7: Exception Handling

Welcome to the land of exception handling in C#. In the perfect world of programming, everything runs smoothly, but let's face it, we don't live in that world. Things go wrong: files don't exist, user inputs are incorrect, networks fail. This is where exception handling steps in, saving the day and ensuring your program can handle unexpected situations gracefully.

At its core, exception handling is about dealing with runtime errors. Instead of letting your program crash when something goes wrong, you catch these errors, or exceptions, and handle them in a controlled way. This process not only makes your programs more robust but also improves the user experience by providing informative error messages instead of abrupt terminations.

In C#, exception handling is managed through the try, catch, and finally blocks. The basic idea is to wrap the code that might throw an exception in a try block, catch the exception with a catch block, and clean up resources with a finally block.

Let's start with the try block. This is where you place the code that might throw an exception. If an exception occurs, the runtime jumps to the corresponding catch block. Here's a simple example:

```
try
  {
```

```
int[] numbers = { 1, 2, 3 };
Console.WriteLine(numbers[5]);
}
catch (IndexOutOfRangeException ex)
{
Console.WriteLine("Index was out of range. Please check the array bounds.");
}
```

In this example, accessing numbers[5] throws an IndexOutOfRangeException because the array only has three elements. The try block catches this exception, and the catch block provides a message to the user.

Catch blocks can catch specific exceptions, as seen above, or more general exceptions. Catching specific exceptions is usually better practice because it allows for more precise error handling. Here's an example of catching a general exception:

```
try
{
int[] numbers = { 1, 2, 3 };
Console.WriteLine(numbers[5]);
}
catch (Exception ex)
{
Console.WriteLine("An error occurred: " + ex.Message);
}
```

In this case, the catch block catches any type of exception, not just IndexOutOfRangeException. While this can be useful in some cases, it's generally better to catch specific exceptions so that you can handle different types of errors appropriately.

The finally block is optional but very useful. It contains code that should run regardless of whether an exception was thrown. This is typically used for cleaning up resources like closing files or releasing network connections. Here's an example:

```csharp
try
  {
  // Open a file and read from it
  }
  catch (IOException ex)
  {
  Console.WriteLine("An I/O error occurred: " + ex.Message);
  }
  finally
  {
  // Close the file
  }
```

In this example, the finally block ensures that the file is closed whether or not an exception was thrown while reading from it.

C# also allows you to throw exceptions explicitly using the throw keyword. This is useful for handling error conditions in your methods and passing the error up the call stack to be handled elsewhere. Here's an example:

```csharp
void CheckAge(int age)
    {
    if (age < 0)
    {
    throw new ArgumentOutOfRangeException("Age cannot be negative.");
    }
    }
```

In this example, if the age parameter is negative, an ArgumentOutOfRangeException is thrown, which can then be caught by the calling code.

Sometimes, you might want to catch an exception, log it, and then rethrow it to be handled by another catch block higher up the call stack. This is done using the throw keyword without any arguments. Here's an example:

```
try
  {
  CheckAge(-5);
  }
  catch (ArgumentOutOfRangeException ex)
  {
  Console.WriteLine("Caught an exception: " + ex.Message);
  throw; // Rethrows the caught exception
  }
```

This technique allows you to handle the exception at multiple levels in your application, providing more detailed logging or user feedback.

C# provides a rich hierarchy of exception classes, all deriving from the System.Exception base class. Some common exception classes include:

- ArgumentException: Thrown when one of the arguments provided to a method is not valid.
    - ArgumentNullException: Thrown when a null argument is passed to a method that does not accept it.
    - InvalidOperationException: Thrown when a method call is invalid for the object's current state.
    - NullReferenceException: Thrown when an attempt is made to dereference a null object reference.
    - DivideByZeroException: Thrown when an attempt is made to divide by zero.

Understanding these common exceptions helps you write more robust code by anticipating and handling potential errors.

Sometimes, it's useful to define your own custom exceptions, particularly when you need to provide more specific error information related to your application. To define a custom exception, create a new class that derives from the Exception class. Here's an example:

```
class CustomException : Exception
    {
    public CustomException(string message) : base(message)
    {
    }
    }
```

In this example, CustomException inherits from Exception and passes a custom error message to the base class constructor. You can then throw and catch this custom exception just like any other exception.

```
try
    {
    throw new CustomException("This is a custom exception.");
    }
    catch (CustomException ex)
    {
    Console.WriteLine("Caught a custom exception: " + ex.Message);
    }
```

Exception handling also plays a crucial role in asynchronous programming. In async methods, exceptions can be caught and handled using try-catch blocks, just as in synchronous methods. However, because async methods return tasks, you also need to consider how exceptions are propagated. Here's an example of an async method with exception handling:

```csharp
async Task DoSomethingAsync()
{
    try
    {
        await Task.Delay(1000);
        throw new InvalidOperationException("An error occurred in the async method.");
    }
    catch (InvalidOperationException ex)
    {
        Console.WriteLine("Caught an exception in async method: " + ex.Message);
    }
}
```

In this example, the exception thrown inside the async method is caught and handled within the same method.

It's also important to handle exceptions that occur in event handlers. Since event handlers are invoked by the runtime, uncaught exceptions can crash your application. To prevent this, wrap the event handler code in a try-catch block. Here's an example:

```csharp
void Button_Click(object sender, EventArgs e)
{
    try
    {
        // Code that might throw an exception
    }
    catch (Exception ex)
    {
        Console.WriteLine("An error occurred: " + ex.Message);
    }
}
```

By wrapping the event handler code in a try-catch block, you ensure that any exceptions are caught and handled, preventing the application from crashing.

Logging exceptions is another critical aspect of error handling. Logging provides a record of what went wrong, which can be invaluable for debugging and improving your application. There are various logging frameworks available for C#, such as NLog, Serilog, and log4net, which make it easy to log exceptions and other information. Here's a simple example using Console.WriteLine for logging:

```
try
  {
  // Code that might throw an exception
  }
  catch (Exception ex)
  {
  Console.WriteLine($"Error: {ex.Message}\nStack Trace: {ex.StackTrace}");
  }
```

In this example, the exception message and stack trace are logged to the console, providing valuable information about the error.

One last thing to consider is the use of exception filters. Exception filters allow you to specify a condition that must be met for the catch block to handle the exception. This can be useful when you need to handle exceptions differently based on certain criteria. Here's an example:

```
try
  {
  // Code that might throw an exception
  }
  catch (Exception ex) when (ex.Message.Contains("specific error"))
```

```
{
    Console.WriteLine("Caught a specific error: " + ex.Message);
}
```

In this example, the catch block only handles exceptions that contain the text "specific error" in their message. This provides more granular control over exception handling.

Exception handling is an essential part of writing robust and reliable C# applications. By understanding how to catch, throw, and log exceptions, you can ensure that your programs handle unexpected situations gracefully and provide a better user experience.

Chapter 8: File I/O and Streams

Welcome to the world of file input/output (I/O) and streams in C#. Handling files is a fundamental aspect of many applications, from reading configuration files to saving user data. Understanding how to work with files and streams is crucial for creating robust and efficient software. This chapter will explore the intricacies of file I/O and streams, providing you with the knowledge to manage data effectively.

File I/O in C# revolves around the System.IO namespace, which offers a comprehensive set of classes for handling files, directories, and streams. Let's start by discussing the basics of reading from and writing to files using some of the key classes provided by this namespace.

The File class is a convenient way to perform common file operations. It provides static methods for creating, copying, deleting, moving, and opening files. For example, to create a new file and write some text to it, you can use the File.WriteAllText method:

```
string path = "example.txt";
   string content = "Hello, File I/O!";
   File.WriteAllText(path, content);
```

In this example, the File.WriteAllText method creates a new file named "example.txt" (or overwrites it if it already exists) and writes the specified content to it. Similarly, you can read the content of a file using the File.ReadAllText method:

```
string readContent = File.ReadAllText(path);
  Console.WriteLine(readContent);
```

This method reads the entire content of the file into a string and prints it to the console. These methods are straightforward and useful for simple file operations, but they load the entire file content into memory, which might not be efficient for large files.

For more advanced file operations, you can use the StreamReader and StreamWriter classes. These classes provide methods for reading and writing text line by line or in chunks, making them more suitable for larger files. Here's an example of how to use StreamWriter to write text to a file:

```
using (StreamWriter writer = new StreamWriter(path))
    {
    writer.WriteLine("Hello, StreamWriter!");
    writer.WriteLine("Writing multiple lines to a file.");
    }
```

In this example, a StreamWriter object is created to write to the specified file. The using statement ensures that the StreamWriter is properly disposed of after use, releasing any resources it holds. The WriteLine method writes a line of text to the file.

To read text from a file using StreamReader, you can use the following code:

```
using (StreamReader reader = new StreamReader(path))
    {
    string line;
    while ((line = reader.ReadLine()) != null)
```

```
    {
    Console.WriteLine(line);
    }
}
```

This example creates a StreamReader object to read from the specified file. The ReadLine method reads each line of the file until the end is reached, and the lines are printed to the console.

Binary files, which contain data in a format not intended for direct human reading, require a different approach. The BinaryReader and BinaryWriter classes are designed for this purpose. These classes allow you to read and write primitive data types as binary values.

Here's an example of writing binary data to a file using BinaryWriter:

```
string binaryPath = "example.bin";
    using (BinaryWriter writer = new BinaryWriter(File.Open(binaryPath, FileMode.Create)))
    {
    writer.Write(1.25);
    writer.Write("BinaryWriter example");
    writer.Write(true);
    }
```

In this example, a BinaryWriter object is created to write to a binary file. The Write methods are used to write a double, a string, and a boolean value to the file.

To read the binary data back from the file using BinaryReader, you can use the following code:

```
using (BinaryReader reader = new BinaryReader(File.Open(binaryPath, File-
```

Mode.Open)))
```
{
double d = reader.ReadDouble();
string s = reader.ReadString();
bool b = reader.ReadBoolean();
Console.WriteLine($"{d}, {s}, {b}");
}
```

This example creates a BinaryReader object to read from the binary file. The Read methods are used to read the data in the same order it was written, and the values are printed to the console.

Streams are another fundamental concept in file I/O. A stream is an abstract representation of a sequence of bytes. Streams provide a way to read and write data sequentially, which is useful for handling data that doesn't fit into memory all at once.

The Stream class is the base class for all streams in C#. There are various derived classes for different types of streams, including FileStream for file operations, MemoryStream for in-memory data, and NetworkStream for network operations.

FileStream is commonly used for file operations where you need more control over reading and writing bytes. Here's an example of writing to a file using FileStream:

```
using (FileStream fileStream = new FileStream(path, FileMode.Create))
{
byte[] data = System.Text.Encoding.UTF8.GetBytes("Hello, FileStream!");
fileStream.Write(data, 0, data.Length);
}
```

In this example, a FileStream object is created to write to the specified file.

The GetBytes method of the Encoding.UTF8 class converts the string to a byte array, which is then written to the file using the Write method.

To read from a file using FileStream, you can use the following code:

```
using (FileStream fileStream = new FileStream(path, FileMode.Open))
{
  byte[] data = new byte[fileStream.Length];
  fileStream.Read(data, 0, data.Length);
  string readContent = System.Text.Encoding.UTF8.GetString(data);
  Console.WriteLine(readContent);
}
```

This example creates a FileStream object to read from the specified file. The Read method reads the bytes from the file into a byte array, which is then converted back to a string using the GetString method of the Encoding.UTF8 class.

MemoryStream is useful for working with data in memory. It can be used to store data temporarily before writing it to a file or transmitting it over a network. Here's an example of using MemoryStream:

```
using (MemoryStream memoryStream = new MemoryStream())
{
  byte[] data = System.Text.Encoding.UTF8.GetBytes("Hello, MemoryStream!");
  memoryStream.Write(data, 0, data.Length);

memoryStream.Seek(0, SeekOrigin.Begin); // Reset the position to the beginning
  byte[] readData = new byte[memoryStream.Length];
  memoryStream.Read(readData, 0, readData.Length);
  string readContent = System.Text.Encoding.UTF8.GetString(readData);
```

```csharp
Console.WriteLine(readContent);
}
```

In this example, a MemoryStream object is used to write data to memory. The Seek method resets the position to the beginning of the stream, allowing the data to be read back.

NetworkStream is used for reading and writing data over network connections. It provides a stream-based interface to network sockets, making it easier to handle network I/O. Here's a basic example of using NetworkStream:

```csharp
using (TcpClient client = new TcpClient("example.com", 80))
{
    using (NetworkStream networkStream = client.GetStream())
    {
        byte[] request = System.Text.Encoding.ASCII.GetBytes("GET / HTTP/1.1\r\nHost: example.com\r\n\r\n");
        networkStream.Write(request, 0, request.Length);

        byte[] response = new byte[1024];
        int bytesRead = networkStream.Read(response, 0, response.Length);
        string responseData = System.Text.Encoding.ASCII.GetString(response, 0, bytesRead);
        Console.WriteLine(responseData);
    }
}
```

In this example, a TcpClient object is created to connect to a web server. A NetworkStream object is obtained from the TcpClient, and a simple HTTP GET request is sent. The response from the server is read and printed to the console.

Working with files and streams is an essential skill for any C# programmer.

Whether you're reading from or writing to files, handling binary data, or working with network streams, the classes provided by the System.IO namespace offer the tools you need to manage data effectively. By understanding these concepts and techniques, you can create applications that interact with the file system and other data sources efficiently and reliably.

Chapter 9: Asynchronous Programming

Welcome to the fascinating world of asynchronous programming in C#. In today's fast-paced, multi-tasking digital environment, creating responsive applications that can handle multiple operations simultaneously is essential. Asynchronous programming is the key to achieving this. It allows your application to perform other tasks while waiting for long-running operations to complete, such as file I/O, network requests, or database queries. This chapter will explore the concepts, benefits, and techniques of asynchronous programming in C#, equipping you with the knowledge to build efficient and responsive applications.

Asynchronous programming in C# revolves around the use of async and await keywords. These keywords, introduced in C# 5.0, make it easier to write asynchronous code that is both readable and maintainable. Before diving into the mechanics of async and await, let's understand the fundamental concepts of synchronous and asynchronous operations.

In a synchronous operation, tasks are performed one after another. The program waits for each task to complete before moving on to the next one. While this is straightforward, it can lead to inefficiencies, particularly when dealing with tasks that take a significant amount of time to complete, such as reading a large file or making a web request.

In contrast, asynchronous operations allow tasks to run concurrently. Instead of waiting for a task to complete, the program can continue executing other tasks. Once the asynchronous task is finished, it notifies the program, and the program can then process the result. This approach improves the responsiveness and performance of applications, especially those that involve I/O-bound or network-bound operations.

Let's start with a simple example to illustrate synchronous versus asynchronous behavior. Here's a synchronous method that reads a file and returns its content as a string:

```
string ReadFile(string path)
{
using (StreamReader reader = new StreamReader(path))
{
return reader.ReadToEnd();
}
}
```

In this synchronous example, the method reads the entire file before returning its content. The calling thread is blocked until the file reading operation completes. This might be fine for small files, but for large files or slow I/O operations, it can make the application unresponsive.

Now, let's convert this method to an asynchronous version using async and await:

```
async Task<string> ReadFileAsync(string path)
{
using (StreamReader reader = new StreamReader(path))
{
return await reader.ReadToEndAsync();
}
}
```

In this asynchronous example, the method returns a Task<string>, representing an ongoing operation that will eventually produce a string result. The await keyword is used to await the completion of the ReadToEndAsync method. While the file is being read, the calling thread can continue executing other tasks. Once the reading operation completes, the result is returned.

To call this asynchronous method, you would use the await keyword as well:

```
async Task ProcessFileAsync(string path)
{
string content = await ReadFileAsync(path);
Console.WriteLine(content);
}
```

The ProcessFileAsync method awaits the completion of the ReadFileAsync method. The calling thread is free to perform other operations while waiting for the file reading to finish, making the application more responsive.

Asynchronous programming isn't limited to file I/O; it's also highly beneficial for network operations, such as making HTTP requests. Here's an example of making an asynchronous HTTP GET request using the HttpClient class:

```
async Task<string> GetWebContentAsync(string url)
{
using (HttpClient client = new HttpClient())
{
HttpResponseMessage response = await client.GetAsync(url);
response.EnsureSuccessStatusCode();
return await response.Content.ReadAsStringAsync();
}
}
```

In this example, the GetWebContentAsync method makes an asynchronous

HTTP GET request to the specified URL. The GetAsync method returns a Task<HttpResponseMessage>, which is awaited. Once the response is received, the EnsureSuccessStatusCode method checks if the request was successful. Finally, the content of the response is read asynchronously using ReadAsStringAsync.

Asynchronous methods can also be composed, meaning you can chain multiple asynchronous operations together. Here's an example of composing asynchronous methods:

```
async Task<string> DownloadAndSaveFileAsync(string url, string path)
  {
  string content = await GetWebContentAsync(url);
  await File.WriteAllTextAsync(path, content);
  return path;
  }
```

In this example, the DownloadAndSaveFileAsync method first calls GetWebContentAsync to download the content from the specified URL. It then saves the content to a file using the asynchronous File.WriteAllTextAsync method. The method returns the path of the saved file once both operations are complete.

One of the key benefits of asynchronous programming is that it allows you to maintain a responsive user interface (UI). In desktop or mobile applications, performing long-running operations on the UI thread can make the application unresponsive, leading to a poor user experience. By offloading these operations to asynchronous methods, the UI thread remains free to handle user interactions.

Here's an example of how you might use asynchronous programming in a Windows Forms application to keep the UI responsive:

```csharp
private async void downloadButton_Click(object sender, EventArgs e)
{
    downloadButton.Enabled = false;
    string url = urlTextBox.Text;
    string path = "downloadedFile.txt";

    try
    {
        await DownloadAndSaveFileAsync(url, path);
        MessageBox.Show("File downloaded successfully!");
    }
    catch (Exception ex)
    {
        MessageBox.Show("An error occurred: " + ex.Message);
    }
    finally
    {
        downloadButton.Enabled = true;
    }
}
```

In this example, when the user clicks the download button, the downloadButton_Click event handler is triggered. This event handler disables the button to prevent multiple clicks, then calls the asynchronous DownloadAndSaveFile Async method. While the file is being downloaded and saved, the UI remains responsive. Once the operation completes, a message box is displayed to inform the user of the result, and the button is re-enabled.

Another important aspect of asynchronous programming is exception handling. Exceptions thrown in asynchronous methods are propagated differently than in synchronous methods. When an exception occurs in an asynchronous method, it is captured and stored in the Task representing the method. You can handle these exceptions using try-catch blocks, just as you would with synchronous code. Here's an example:

```
async Task<string> GetWebContentWithErrorHandlingAsync(string url)
{
try
{
using (HttpClient client = new HttpClient())
{
HttpResponseMessage response = await client.GetAsync(url);
response.EnsureSuccessStatusCode();
return await response.Content.ReadAsStringAsync();
}
}
catch (HttpRequestException ex)
{
Console.WriteLine("An HTTP error occurred: " + ex.Message);
return null;
}
catch (Exception ex)
{
Console.WriteLine("An unexpected error occurred: " + ex.Message);
return null;
}
}
```

In this example, exceptions thrown during the HTTP request are caught and handled within the asynchronous method. Specific exceptions, such as HttpRequestException, are caught first, followed by a general Exception catch block for any other exceptions.

Understanding how to properly await asynchronous operations is crucial for avoiding common pitfalls such as deadlocks. One common mistake is using the Result property or Wait method on a Task, which blocks the calling thread and defeats the purpose of asynchronous programming. Instead, always use the await keyword to wait for the completion of an asynchronous operation.

It's also worth noting that not all APIs in the .NET Framework are asynchronous. However, many have been updated to support asynchronous programming. When working with APIs that do not support async, you can run them asynchronously using the Task.Run method, which offloads the work to a background thread. Here's an example:

```csharp
async Task<string> ReadFileOnBackgroundThreadAsync(string path)
{
return await Task.Run(() =>
{
using (StreamReader reader = new StreamReader(path))
{
return reader.ReadToEnd();
}
});
}
```

In this example, the file reading operation is run on a background thread using Task.Run, allowing the calling thread to remain responsive.

Asynchronous programming in C# is a powerful technique that enhances the performance and responsiveness of your applications. By leveraging async and await, you can write code that efficiently handles long-running operations without blocking the main thread. Whether you're working with file I/O, network requests, or any other time-consuming tasks, asynchronous programming is an essential tool in your C# programming toolkit. Understanding and mastering these concepts will enable you to build modern, responsive, and efficient applications.

Chapter 10: Advanced Topics and Best Practices

Welcome to the world of advanced topics and best practices in C#. This chapter delves into some sophisticated aspects of C# programming, sharing techniques that will help you write better, more maintainable code. By understanding and applying these advanced concepts, you can enhance your C# skills significantly.

One advanced feature in C# is the use of delegates. Delegates are types that represent references to methods. They are used to pass methods as arguments to other methods, enabling flexible and reusable code. A delegate can point to a method that matches its signature. Here's an example of defining and using a delegate:

```csharp
public delegate void DisplayMessage(string message);

void ShowMessage(string message)
  {
  Console.WriteLine(message);
  }

DisplayMessage displayMessageDelegate = ShowMessage;
  displayMessageDelegate("Hello, Delegates!");
```

In this example, the DisplayMessage delegate is defined to reference methods that take a string parameter and return void. The ShowMessage method matches this signature, so it can be assigned to the delegate. When the delegate is invoked, it calls the ShowMessage method.

Events are a special type of delegate used for handling events. They provide a way for a class to notify other classes or objects when something of interest happens. Events follow the publisher-subscriber model. Here's an example of using events:

```csharp
public class Alarm
    {
    public event Action OnAlarmRaised;

public void RaiseAlarm()
    {
    OnAlarmRaised?.Invoke();
    }
    }

public class AlarmListener
    {
    public void Subscribe(Alarm alarm)
    {
    alarm.OnAlarmRaised += () => Console.WriteLine("Alarm raised!");
    }
    }
```

In this example, the Alarm class defines an event called OnAlarmRaised, which is triggered when the RaiseAlarm method is called. The AlarmListener class subscribes to this event and prints a message when the event is raised.

Another advanced feature is lambda expressions, which provide a concise way to represent anonymous methods. They are particularly useful in scenarios where you need to pass a simple method as a parameter. Lambda expressions are often used with LINQ (Language Integrated Query) to manipulate collections. Here's an example of using a lambda expression:

```
List<int> numbers = new List<int> { 1, 2, 3, 4, 5 };
  List<int> evenNumbers = numbers.Where(n => n % 2 == 0).ToList();
```

In this example, the lambda expression n => n % 2 == 0 is used to filter the list of numbers, selecting only the even numbers. The Where method applies the lambda expression to each element in the list, and the ToList method converts the result back to a list.

Generics are another powerful feature in C#. They allow you to define classes, methods, and interfaces with placeholders for the types they operate on. This provides type safety and reduces code duplication. Here's an example of a generic class:

```
public class GenericList<T>
  {
  private List<T> items = new List<T>();

public void Add(T item)
  {
  items.Add(item);
  }

public T Get(int index)
  {
  return items[index];
  }
  }
```

In this example, the GenericList class can hold items of any type specified by the type parameter T. The Add method adds an item to the list, and the Get method retrieves an item by index. You can create instances of the GenericList class with different types:

GenericList<int> intList = new GenericList<int>();
  intList.Add(1);
  int number = intList.Get(0);

GenericList<string> stringList = new GenericList<string>();
  stringList.Add("Hello");
  string text = stringList.Get(0);

Design patterns are best practices for solving common software design problems. They provide proven solutions and help create more flexible, reusable, and maintainable code. Some popular design patterns in C# include the Singleton, Factory, and Observer patterns.

The Singleton pattern ensures that a class has only one instance and provides a global point of access to it. Here's an example of the Singleton pattern:

public class Singleton
  {
  private static Singleton instance;

private Singleton() { }

public static Singleton Instance
  {
  get
  {
  if (instance == null)
  {

```
    instance = new Singleton();
  }
  return instance;
  }
 }
}
```

In this example, the Singleton class has a private constructor to prevent direct instantiation. The Instance property returns the single instance of the class, creating it if necessary.

The Factory pattern provides a way to create objects without specifying the exact class of the object that will be created. This is useful for encapsulating object creation logic. Here's an example of the Factory pattern:

```
public interface IProduct
  {
  void Use();
  }

public class ConcreteProductA : IProduct
  {
  public void Use()
  {
  Console.WriteLine("Using Product A");
  }
  }

public class ConcreteProductB : IProduct
  {
  public void Use()
  {
  Console.WriteLine("Using Product B");
```

```csharp
    }
}

public class ProductFactory
{
    public IProduct CreateProduct(string type)
    {
        switch (type)
        {
            case "A":
                return new ConcreteProductA();
            case "B":
                return new ConcreteProductB();
            default:
                throw new ArgumentException("Invalid product type");
        }
    }
}
```

In this example, the ProductFactory class creates instances of IProduct based on the specified type. This encapsulates the object creation logic and allows for easy extension by adding new product types.

The Observer pattern defines a one-to-many dependency between objects, so that when one object changes state, all its dependents are notified and updated automatically. Here's an example of the Observer pattern:

```csharp
public interface IObserver
{
    void Update();
}

public class Subject
```

```csharp
{
    private List<IObserver> observers = new List<IObserver>();

    public void Attach(IObserver observer)
    {
        observers.Add(observer);
    }

    public void Detach(IObserver observer)
    {
        observers.Remove(observer);
    }

    public void Notify()
    {
        foreach (var observer in observers)
        {
            observer.Update();
        }
    }
}

public class ConcreteObserver : IObserver
{
    public void Update()
    {
        Console.WriteLine("Observer notified.");
    }
}
```

In this example, the Subject class maintains a list of observers and provides methods to attach and detach observers. When the Notify method is called, all attached observers are notified by calling their Update method.

Reflection is another advanced topic in C#. It allows you to inspect and interact with object types at runtime. This is useful for tasks like dynamically loading assemblies, invoking methods, or accessing properties without knowing their names at compile time. Here's an example of using reflection to invoke a method:

```csharp
public class MyClass
  {
  public void MyMethod()
  {
  Console.WriteLine("MyMethod called.");
  }
  }

Type type = typeof(MyClass);
    object instance = Activator.CreateInstance(type);
    MethodInfo method = type.GetMethod("MyMethod");
    method.Invoke(instance, null);
```

In this example, the Type class is used to obtain metadata about MyClass. The Activator.CreateInstance method creates an instance of MyClass, and the GetMethod and Invoke methods are used to call the MyMethod method.

Another important best practice is understanding and implementing solid principles. These principles help create more understandable, flexible, and maintainable code. The solid acronym stands for:

1. Single Responsibility Principle: A class should have only one reason to change, meaning it should have only one job or responsibility.

2. Open/Closed Principle: Classes should be open for extension but closed for modification. This means you should be able to add new functionality without changing existing code.

3. Liskov Substitution Principle: Subtypes must be substitutable for their base types. This ensures that derived classes can be used in place of their base classes without altering the correctness of the program.

4. Interface Segregation Principle: Clients should not be forced to depend on interfaces they do not use. This means designing interfaces that are specific to the needs of the clients.

5. Dependency Inversion Principle: High-level modules should not depend on low-level modules. Both should depend on abstractions. This promotes loose coupling between classes and enhances code maintainability.

Understanding and applying these principles can significantly improve the quality of your code and make it easier to maintain and extend.

Unit testing is another crucial aspect of writing robust and reliable software. Unit tests validate that individual parts of your application work as expected. By writing tests for your code, you can catch bugs early and ensure that changes do not break existing functionality. Frameworks like NUnit, MSTest, and xUnit provide tools for writing and running unit tests in C#. Here's a simple example of a unit test using NUnit:

```
[TestFixture]
    public class CalculatorTests
    {
    [Test]
    public void Add_AddsTwoNumbers_ReturnsSum()
    {
    // Arrange
    var calculator = new Calculator();

// Act
    var result = calculator.Add(2, 3);
```

```
// Assert
  Assert.AreEqual(5, result);
  }
}
```

In this example, the CalculatorTests class contains a test method that verifies the Add method of the Calculator class. The [Test] attribute marks the method as a test, and the Assert.AreEqual method checks that the result is as expected.

Code review is another best practice that helps maintain code quality. By having peers review your code, you can catch potential issues, improve code readability, and share knowledge within the team. Code reviews encourage collaboration and help ensure that the codebase remains clean and maintainable.

Documentation is also vital. Well-documented code is easier to understand and maintain. Use XML comments to document your classes, methods, and properties. This provides context and explanations for your code, making it easier for others (and yourself) to work with it in the future.

By mastering these advanced topics and best practices, you can create more efficient, maintainable, and robust applications in C#. These concepts and techniques form the foundation of

professional software development, enabling you to tackle complex challenges and build high-quality software.

Conclusion: Your Next Steps in C# Mastery

As we reach the end of our journey through C# programming, it's a great moment to reflect on the rich tapestry of concepts, tools, and techniques we've covered. From the fundamentals to advanced topics, we've built a solid foundation for mastering C# and developing robust applications. This conclusion will serve as a comprehensive review of what you've learned and highlight the broader context of how these skills fit into the world of software development.

Let's start by revisiting the basics. The journey began with understanding what C# is and setting up the development environment. C#, developed by Microsoft, is a powerful, modern, and object-oriented programming language that has become a cornerstone of the .NET ecosystem. Visual Studio and Visual Studio Code are the primary tools we use to write, debug, and manage our C# projects. They provide an integrated development environment that makes coding in C# efficient and enjoyable.

We then moved on to variables, data types, and operators. These are the fundamental building blocks of any program. Variables store data that can change, while constants hold data that remains the same throughout the program. Understanding data types, such as integers, floating-point numbers, characters, strings, and Booleans, is crucial for effective programming. Operators allow us to perform operations on these data types, from basic arithmetic to more complex logical and comparison operations.

Control structures, including conditional statements and loops, were our next stop. Conditional statements like if, else if, and else enable the program to make decisions based on certain conditions. Loops, such as for, while, and do-while, allow us to execute a block of code repeatedly, which is essential for tasks like processing collections of data. Mastering these control structures is key to writing dynamic and responsive programs.

Methods and functions were another critical topic. Methods encapsulate code into reusable blocks, making our programs more modular and easier to manage. We explored how to define methods, pass parameters, return values, and use method overloading and recursion. Understanding methods and functions is fundamental to writing clean, efficient, and maintainable code.

Object-oriented programming (OOP) was a significant milestone in our journey. OOP principles, such as encapsulation, inheritance, polymorphism, and abstraction, provide a framework for building complex applications. Encapsulation protects the internal state of objects, inheritance allows us to create new classes based on existing ones, polymorphism enables us to use objects of different types interchangeably, and abstraction hides implementation details, exposing only the essential features.

We then delved into arrays and collections. Arrays are fixed-size collections of elements, while collections, such as lists, dictionaries, queues, and stacks, provide more flexible and dynamic ways to manage groups of data. Understanding how to use these data structures effectively is crucial for handling data in our applications.

Exception handling was another vital topic. Exceptions are runtime errors that can disrupt the normal flow of a program. Using try, catch, and finally blocks, we can catch and handle these exceptions, ensuring our programs can gracefully recover from errors. This is essential for creating robust and user-friendly applications.

CONCLUSION: YOUR NEXT STEPS IN C# MASTERY

File I/O and streams were next on our list. File I/O allows us to read from and write to files, while streams provide a way to process data sequentially. We explored the use of classes like File, StreamReader, StreamWriter, BinaryReader, and BinaryWriter, which are essential for managing data stored in files. Understanding these concepts is crucial for applications that need to persist data or interact with the file system.

Asynchronous programming was another advanced topic we tackled. Using async and await keywords, we can write code that performs long-running operations without blocking the main thread. This is especially important for creating responsive applications that can handle tasks like file I/O, network requests, and database queries efficiently. Understanding asynchronous programming is essential for modern software development.

Finally, we explored advanced topics and best practices. This included delegates, events, lambda expressions, generics, design patterns, reflection, and solid principles. These concepts help us write more flexible, reusable, and maintainable code. Understanding and applying these advanced topics is crucial for professional software development.

Delegates are types that represent references to methods, enabling flexible and reusable code. Events are a special type of delegate used for handling events, providing a way for a class to notify other classes or objects when something of interest happens. Lambda expressions offer a concise way to represent anonymous methods, often used with LINQ to manipulate collections.

Generics allow us to define classes, methods, and interfaces with placeholders for the types they operate on, providing type safety and reducing code duplication. Design patterns, such as the Singleton, Factory, and Observer patterns, provide proven solutions to common software design problems, promoting flexibility, reusability, and maintainability.

Reflection allows us to inspect and interact with object types at runtime, useful for tasks like dynamically loading assemblies or invoking methods without knowing their names at compile time. Solid principles guide us in writing more understandable, flexible, and maintainable code. These principles include the Single Responsibility Principle, Open/Closed Principle, Liskov Substitution Principle, Interface Segregation Principle, and Dependency Inversion Principle.

Unit testing is another best practice that helps maintain code quality. By writing tests for our code, we can catch bugs early and ensure that changes do not break existing functionality. Frameworks like NUnit, MSTest, and xUnit provide tools for writing and running unit tests in C#. Code review is another best practice that helps maintain code quality by having peers review our code. This encourages collaboration and ensures that the codebase remains clean and maintainable.

Documentation is also vital. Well-documented code is easier to understand and maintain. Using XML comments to document our classes, methods, and properties provides context and explanations for our code, making it easier for others (and ourselves) to work with it in the future.

Understanding these advanced topics and best practices is crucial for creating more efficient, maintainable, and robust applications in C#. These concepts and techniques form the foundation of professional software development, enabling us to tackle complex challenges and build high-quality software.

As we review the journey through C# programming, it's clear that the language offers a rich set of features and tools for building a wide variety of applications. From basic syntax and data types to advanced topics like asynchronous programming and design patterns, C# provides a robust framework for developing modern software.

Mastering C# requires a deep understanding of its features and best practices. By continually learning and applying these concepts, we can create applications that are efficient, maintainable, and scalable. This knowledge not only makes us better C# developers but also prepares us for the broader challenges of software development in an ever-evolving industry.

Understanding the depth and breadth of C# programming is essential for any developer looking to build robust and scalable applications. From handling data efficiently with arrays and collections to writing responsive and user-friendly applications with asynchronous programming, C# equips us with the tools we need to succeed. The journey through C# programming is one of continuous learning and improvement, with each concept building on the previous ones to create a comprehensive understanding of the language and its capabilities. This journey through the intricacies of C# programming has laid a strong foundation for your future endeavors in software development. The knowledge and skills you've gained here will be invaluable as you continue to build, refine, and innovate with C#.

www.ingramcontent.com/pod-product-compliance
Lightning Source LLC
Chambersburg PA
CBHW070312230526
45470CB00002B/838